ALISON HOLST'S
BEST POTATO
RECIPES

First published 1995 by Hyndman
Publishing PO Box 5017, Dunedin.
© Text: Alison Holst
Designers: Rob Di Leva
Production: Di Leva Design
Illustrator: Clare Ferguson
Photography: Sal Criscillo
Home Economists: Alison Holst, Jane
Ritchie, Dee Harris
Editorial Assistant: Keryn Wear
Printing: Tablet Printing Company

1st Printing March 1995   (15,000 copies)
1st Reprint April 1995   (5,000 copies)
2nd Reprint Sept. 1995   (5,000 copies)
3rd Reprint Nov. 1995   (21,000 copies)
4th Reprint Nov. 1995   (10,000 copies)

Acknowledgements

ALISON'S CHOICE for bulk whole foods

ACTON INTERNATIONAL
MARKETING LTD for Kikkoman Soya
Sauce, Trappey's Pepper Sauce, Samoa Fia Fia
Coconut Cream, Lorea Anchovies and
bottled Golden Sun Red Peppers

BARKERS FRUIT PROCESSORS LTD for
preserves

BENNICKS POULTRY FARM, Levin for
fresh eggs

COUNTRY FOODS (N.Z.) LTD for
Country Goodness Sour Cream and Cream
Cheese, Anchor Grated Tasty Cheddar, Swiss
Maid Yoghurt

EMPIRE FOODSTUFFS for dried herbs,
spices and seasoned salts

FERNDALE DAIRIES for speciality cheeses

HARKNESS & YOUNG for Willow and
Probus cookware

J. WATTIE FOODS for canned fruit, fish,
vegetables and tomato products

LAMNEI PLASTICS, Lower Hutt for
Alison Holst's Microwave Dishes

NESTLE NEW ZEALAND LTD for instant
stocks

NEW ZEALAND PORK INDUSTRY
BOARD for bacon

PARKVALE MUSHROOMS

RICHMOND FOODS for New Way Pastry

SEASMOKE for smoked salmon

S.C. JOHNSON & SON PTY LIMITED
for Chef Mate

TEGEL FOODS LTD for chicken and
turkey

TIMOS FILO PASTRY

WILLIAM AITKEN & CO. for Azalea
Grapeseed Oil and Lupi Olive Oil

YUM PRODUCTS for mustards and nut
butters

COVER PHOTOGRAPH: *Jacket Wedges page 10*

Contents

Before you start

In this book I have often referred to potatoes by size. A small new potato weighs about 50 grams. A small maincrop potato weighs about 100 grams. A medium maincrop potato weighs about 150 grams. A large maincrop potato weighs 200 – 250 grams.

Unless potatoes are described as new, use maincrop potato in the recipes.

In potato cookery, you seldom need to be precise about weights, but the weights given above may help you if you want to use, say, one large potato instead of two small ones.

Use fresh herbs when *fresh* is specified, otherwise use dried herbs except for parsley.

When *coconut cream* is listed in any recipe, use standard or lower-fat canned coconut cream. (Freeze leftover canned coconut cream in quantities to suit, for later use.)

A 720 Watt microwave oven was used to cook the microwaved foods in this book. Microwave cooking times are given as a guide only. Alter times to suit the wattage of the microwave oven you use.

For best results, use a standard metric (250 ml) measuring cup and metric measuring spoons when you use these recipes.
1 tablespoon holds 15 ml.
1 teaspoon holds 5 ml.

All the cup and spoon measures in the recipes are level, unless otherwise stated.

Sets of measuring cups make it easier to measure ¼ and ½ cup quantities.

Large amounts of butter are given by weight. Butter packs usually have 50 gram or 100 gram markings on them. Small amounts of butter are measured by spoons. One tablespoon of butter weighs 15 grams.

cm	centimeter
C	Celsius
ml	millilitre
g	gram
tsp	teaspoon
Tbsp	tablespoon

Potatoes Please

I can't imagine cooking family meals without potatoes.

My first responsibilities in the kitchen, as a child, involved draining, mashing and serving the potatoes which we ate every evening, along with meat and two or three other vegetables.

My cooking and eating patterns have changed a great deal since this time, and many new foods have appeared on our table, but potatoes which we grow or buy, and eat regularly, are still an important part of our family food.

Why? Because everybody, young and old, *likes* potatoes, whether they are served as a small part of dinner, or the main part of another meal.

Also because they are such good value, economically and nutritionally, I feel that potatoes should be served often in any low-cost food plan.

And of course, as this book will show you, potatoes are also very versatile.

Never underestimate the popularity of potatoes. I worked with the Potato Board for many years, and during this time packed a record 970 people into a hall at one end of the country, and 860

people at the other. All paid about $10 for charity, and came to see potatoes being cooked! When I talk about potatoes on radio, there are four times as many requests for potato recipes as there are for others. And, last year, after one of my potato recipes was published in a local newspaper, that city sold out of one of the required ingredients.

I don't think I have ever written a book which contains so few ingredients. Most cooks will find that they already have what they need to make these recipes in their storecupboard or refrigerator — a real bonus!

The recipes included in this book are my own tried and true favourites. I am sure that you will enjoy making and eating them too.

Everyday Potatoes

Plain Potatoes

Cut peeled potatoes into evenly sized pieces. Drop into boiling water. Cover pot, so potatoes are surrounded by water or steam. When water boils, lower heat so water barely simmers. Cook 15-40 minutes until tender when pierced. Drain.

New potatoes - scrape, or peel a band around centre of each small potato. Add a little sugar, salt, mint sprigs, garlic or other herbs. After water boils, cook very gently in water to cover until tender when pierced. Drain immediately.

TO MICROWAVE: Put old and new potatoes in oven bags, loosely closed with a rubber band. Cut into even pieces. Add 2–3 teaspoons water and $1/2$ teaspoon butter or olive oil per serving. See page 18 for cooking times. Turn bag once during cooking.

Mashed Potatoes

Cook peeled potatoes in a small amount of boiling salted water until soft, in a covered pot. Drain, stand for 2–3 minutes, add 1 teaspoon butter per serving then mash. For a creamy consistency, beat with a fork adding milk and seasoning as needed. Serve immediately.

TO MICROWAVE: Cut peeled potatoes each into small, even pieces. Add 1 teaspoon butter and 1 tablespoon water per serving. Cover and microwave on High for 2–3 minutes per serving. Shake half-way through cooking time. Leave to stand 5 minutes, then mash without draining, adding milk, salt and pepper to taste. Beat with a fork after mashing.

Duchesse Potatoes

For best results use floury potatoes. For four servings boil 5 small (500g) peeled potatoes cut into evenly sized pieces (see boiled potatoes recipe). When tender, but not mushy, press through a sieve or potato ricer then mash with 25g butter and a large beaten egg (and an extra yolk if possible). Keep mixture firm. Season to taste then pipe rosettes on to a greased (or sprayed) baking tray using a forcer bag with a star nozzle.

Bake at 200°C for 20 minutes or until edges turn brown. Rosettes spread a little when baked.

VARIATION: Pipe rings instead of rosettes. After browning fill with mushrooms, peas etc.

Everyday Potatoes

Hash Browns

Boil potatoes until barely tender, refrigerate at least 8 hours, then grate coarsely. Spoon into preheated pan containing a film of butter heated to straw colour. Pat lightly down to form a cake. Brown over moderate heat for 10–15 minutes, until a crisp crust forms.

Slide out of pan onto a plate. Flip back into pan, uncooked side down. Slip extra butter down sides of pan and cook second side to the same stage.

Skillet Potatoes

For 3–4 servings:

Scrub or peel 4 medium potatoes (600g), then slice 5mm thick. Drop into cold water.

Cook 2 sliced onions in 3–4 tablespoons butter in a non-stick fry pan with a lid. Drain the potatoes, pat dry and add to the onions. Turn to coat with butter. Cover and cook over low heat for 15 minutes, turning occasionally.

Uncover, then turn up the heat a little and allow vegetables to brown slightly, cooking for 10–15 minutes longer.

Just before serving, drain off any excess butter, season with salt and pepper, and sprinkle with 2 tablespoons chopped parsley.

Birdsnest Potatoes

Grate 1 large scrubbed potato per person onto an old teatowel. Squeeze cloth to remove liquid, then drop handfuls of potato into a very hot frypan containing a little oil. Flatten lightly, but do not pack down. Turn when golden, adding more oil if necessary.

NOTE: Work fast, since potatoes brown on standing.

Everyday Potatoes

Oven-Baked Potatoes

TO BAKE TRADITIONALLY: Scrub medium to large potatoes then coat with oil to keep skins soft. Bake, on rack, at 200°C for 50–60 minutes, or at 180°C for 60–75 minutes, until soft when pressed.

TO MICROWAVE ON HIGH:
For 100g allow 3 minutes
For 200g allow 5½ minutes
For 300g allow 7½–8 minutes
For 400g allow 10 minutes

Prick each scrubbed potato several times before cooking. Turn potatoes over half-way through cooking time.

After standing, cut a cross in the top of each potato and press down between the cuts to open out the cross. Put a little butter, sour cream or cheese in the cut.

Baked Potato Skins

Quarter baked potatoes lengthwise. Scoop or cut out flesh, leaving ½ cm of potato on skins. (Use flesh for other recipes.) Brush with oil. Season with salt and pepper. Bake in a shallow metal dish, at 230°C for 15–20 minutes, or until crisp and browned around edges. Top or dip as desired, with Salsa, Pesto, Pizza toppings, mushrooms etc.

Roast Potatoes

Potatoes roasted in the oven with meat need little attention. They take about 60–75 minutes at 180°C. Turn occasionally to crisp all sides.

For Crusty Roast potatoes, parboil as below, pat dry, coat lightly with flour then roast as above.

For Garlic Roast Potatoes peel and boil in salted water to cover, for 5 minutes, then drain and cool enough to handle. Squash 2 cloves garlic in ¼ cup oil. Make crosswise cuts in potatoes, 5mm apart, nearly to base. Stand in shallow baking dish and cook at 200°C for about an hour brushing with garlic oil at intervals.

Everyday Potatoes

Easy Chips

When you bake chips instead of frying them, you use much less oil.

For 2–3 servings: Peel or scrub 2–3 large potatoes (500g) and slice them thinly into chips 5mm thick. Drop the chips into a bowl of cold water straight after they are cut. Rinse, then pat dry. Dry bowl, and add chips. Pour 2–3 tablespoons oil over them and mix with fingers until completely coated.

Lie chips in one layer in a sponge roll tin or roasting pan. Bake at 230°C for 20 minutes, until tender, turning once. If chips do not brown in this time, brown them under a hot grill. Sprinkle with salt and serve soon after cooking.

Scalloped Potatoes

For 3–4 servings:

Slice 4 medium potatoes (600g) thinly into cold water. Drain and arrange in a shallow ovenware dish. Heat together in a pot 1 cup milk, 2 tablespoons butter, 1 teaspoon salt, pepper and a thinly sliced garlic clove. When bubbling pour over potatoes. Cover and bake at 200°C for 30 minutes, then uncover and bake 15–30 minutes longer, until top is golden brown.

Sauteed Potatoes

For 2 servings:

Slice 3–4 medium-sized (500g) cold, cooked new potatoes into chunky pieces. Heat 3–4 tablespoons of butter or oil in a non-stick frypan. When hot add the potatoes and cook uncovered, turning occasionally for 20–40 minutes, until evenly crisp and golden. Sprinkle with chopped parsley before serving.

VARIATION: In a small pan, bring to boil 2 tablespoons wine vinegar, 1 chopped garlic clove, 1 teaspoon finely grated lemon rind and 2 tablespoons olive oil. Pour over sauteed potatoes before serving.

Jacket Wedges

These trendy snacks are popular with all age groups. Ring in the changes by adding different spices to flavour them, then serve with one or more bought or homemade dips — the sky's the limit!

For 3–4 servings:

4 large potatoes (1kg)
3 Tbsp olive oil
1 Tbsp light soya sauce
1 tsp very finely chopped garlic
1 Tbsp grated Parmesan cheese
½ tsp salt

Scrub potatoes, but do not peel. Cut each potato into about 8 wedges, lengthwise. Put the wedges into a bowl of cold water to rinse them. Drain and pat dry.

In a bowl, mix together the olive oil, soya sauce, garlic, Parmesan and salt. Using your fingers, gently turn the dried potatoes in this mixture to coat them thoroughly. Stand the wedges, skin side down in a large baking dish.

Bake at 200°C for 35–40 minutes, or until tender and golden brown.

VARIATIONS: Mix other seasonings with the oil, to suit your taste.

❦ Serve hot or warm with dips such as guacamole, salsa, satay sauce, or sour cream, as snacks or appetisers.

Sinfully Rich Potato Wedges

These rich but absolutely delicious potatoes should be served only as an occasional treat.
They are coated with a heavily herbed and spiced mixture and baked until crisp —WONDERFUL!

For 3–4 servings:

4 large potatoes (1kg)
25g butter, melted
¼ tsp salt
3 Tbsp olive oil
2 tsp finely chopped garlic
2 tsp ground cumin
1 tsp dried oreganum
¼ –½ tsp chili powder

Microwave or boil scrubbed potatoes until barely tender. Cool if you have time, then cut potatoes lengthwise, each into 8 wedges.

Soften butter in a large roasting pan. Add salt, olive oil, garlic, cumin, oreganum and chili and mix well.

Turn the potato wedges in the roasting pan, mixing gently but thoroughly with your hands until potatoes are well coated. Spread in a single layer, then bake at 180°C for 1–1½ hours, until crispy, turning once.

VARIATION: Vary the amounts and types of herbs and spices used to suit yourself.

❦ Serve warm, as a snack, for dipping into your favourite tomato-based salsa.

Mediterranean Potatoes

This recipe turns everyday potatoes into something which will delight everybody who eats them! Depending on the flavourings added, these potatoes can be served "on the side", or as the main part of a casual meal.

For 2 main course servings:

6 medium potatoes (900g)
2–3 Tbsp olive or other oil
1–2 large cloves garlic
chili powder
    OR cayenne pepper
several sprigs of fresh thyme,
    rosemary or sage
½ tsp salt
    OR 2 tsp chopped capers
1 Tbsp chopped anchovies
2 Tbsp caper vinegar
about ¼ cup chopped parsley
black olives (optional)

Scrub the potatoes to remove all dirt, then cut lengthwise into large chunky wedges or chip shapes. Rinse or stand in cold water, pat dry.

Heat the oil in a large frypan, add the prepared potatoes, and toss to coat. Cover the pan and cook over a moderate heat, turning every five minutes for about 20 minutes, until potatoes are barely tender, and lightly browned on most sides. While turning the second time, add the finely chopped garlic, sprinkle the potatoes with chili powder or cayenne pepper then mix well. Put several sprigs of your chosen herb and the salt or capers in the pan on top of the potatoes before you put the lid back on. As soon as the potatoes are tender,

remove the herbs, add the anchovies and caper vinegar and cook about 10 minutes longer with the lid off, turning occasionally. Adjust the seasonings. Mix the chopped parsley through the potatoes just before serving.

Pile in serving dish and scatter the olives (if used) over the top.

🐦 Serve bowls of warm or hot potatoes with poached eggs and a green salad. Good with a chunky tomato and basil salad, too.

Mediterranean Potatoes

Friggione

Friggione

For this recipe to be at its best, do not hurry its cooking time. Although it loses its bright colour, it tastes better and better as the liquid disappears, and the mixture browns.

For 4–6 servings:

about ¼ cup olive oil
5 medium potatoes, cubed (750g)
2 large red onions
2 red or green peppers
425g can Italian Seasoned Tomatoes
1– 1½ tsp salt
1 tsp sugar
freshly ground black pepper
chopped parsley (optional)

Heat the oil in a large frypan, preferably one with a non-stick surface. Cut the potatoes into 1 cm cubes and slice the onions and peppers.

Add potatoes, onions and peppers to the hot oil. Cover and cook over a moderate heat for 20 minutes, stirring several times, until the vegetables are tender and lightly browned.

Add the tomatoes and their juice. Cook uncovered over a medium heat for 15–30 minutes until the mixture darkens in colour and has reduced, so there is only a small amount of liquid around the potatoes. Season to taste and sprinkle with chopped parsley before serving.

❦ Serve warm or hot, reheating in the frypan if necessary. Excellent alone, or as part of a barbecue or buffet meal. Good with ham or smoked chicken too.

Nelson Potatoes

This is a really good recipe I dreamed up one stormy night in Nelson.
As it is so delicious, always cook considerably more than you think you will need.

For 4 servings:

2 medium onions
2 Tbsp butter or oil
3 medium apples
3 large potatoes, sliced (600g)
½ cup liquid (see below)
pepper and salt
chopped fresh herbs

Peel and slice the onions. Cook in a large frypan in the butter or oil until transparent and browned on the edges. Raise the heat, add the sliced apples and cook uncovered, stirring often, until the apples have browned slightly, too.

Mix in the sliced potatoes, then add the liquid. (Use apple juice, instant stock and water, or wine). Cover pan tightly and cook for about 20 minutes until potatoes are tender. Turn occasionally, adding extra liquid if the mixture becomes too dry.

Add freshly ground pepper, salt and chopped sage, thyme or oreganum to taste, just before serving.

❦ Served with sausages or pork chops it is especially good, but we like it with any grilled meat, as well as ham and smoked chicken.

Potato Cakes

Deservedly popular, these potato cakes don't need to be made to an exact formula - vary their seasonings and additions each time you make them, using what is available.

For 1–2 servings:

1 cup grated or mashed cold cooked potato
¹/₂ cup self-raising flour or scone mix
¹/₂ tsp celery salt
¹/₂ tsp green herb stock
about 2 Tbsp chopped parsley or other herbs
up to ¹/₂ cup chopped cooked vegetables, chicken or meat (optional)
milk

Coarsely grate or mash boiled or microwaved potatoes and mix with next 4 or 5 ingredients. Add enough milk to mix to a firm dough. Form into a cylinder on a wooden board, using more flour to prevent it sticking. Cut into 1cm slices using a sharp (serrated) knife. Lightly flour the cut surfaces of each potato cake. (Mixture turns sticky if left to stand, so cook immediately).

Cook 4–5 minutes per side until evenly browned in a pan containing 5mm hot oil. Do not shorten the cooking time or the centres of the potato cakes will be pasty. Always heat oil before adding potato cakes.

VARIATIONS: For fish cakes drain a can of tuna or salmon, keeping the liquid. Leave out the celery salt and instant stock and mix cakes using the reserved liquid before adding milk. For a milder flavour discard the liquid from the can and use flavourings and milk as above.

❦ Serve hot for breakfast or lunch or with other foods for dinner.

Microwaved Cubed Potatoes

Additions before cooking mean no last minute fuss when serving. This a very useful way to precook potatoes for salads and other recipes. After you have seen how well the basic method works, vary the seasonings and the shapes of the pieces to suit yourself.

For 1 serving:

1 medium potato, cubed
   (125 –150g)
½ tsp butter or oil
2 tsp water
½ clove garlic, chopped
   OR 2 tsp chopped parsley
   OR 1 spring onion, chopped
   OR 1 mint sprig

Scrub or peel potatoes. Cut in 15mm cubes, dropping these into a bowl of cold water as prepared.

Drain and put in an oven bag or small microwave dish. Add remaining ingredients, using oil if potatoes will be used in a salad. The potatoes will cook fastest, and most evenly if they almost fill the container they are in. An unpunctured oven bag is best, because you can (loosely) fasten it with a rubber band close to the potatoes, trapping little air. (Such a bag can be used many times.)

Approximate cooking times on High:
1 serving (125–150g) 3–3½ minutes
2 servings (250–300g) 4–4½ minutes
4 servings (500–600g) 5–6½ minutes

During cooking shake container to coat potato pieces evenly with butter and seasonings after butter melts. Squeeze bag to see if the potatoes are done. As soon as they "give" stop cooking.

Allow a standing time of 3–4 minutes after cooking.

NOTE: If potatoes are hard they are undercooked. If they are shrunken, they have overcooked.

❦ Serve as is, use in salads, or in dishes requiring cooked potatoes.

Crunchy Brown Microwaved Potatoes

These are as close as I can get to fried potatoes in a microwave. If you heat the browning dish properly I think you will find the results are remarkably good. Change the seasonings to suit yourself, but add some curry powder and paprika to get a good colour.

For 2 servings:

2 medium potatoes (300g)
1 Tbsp flour
1 tsp salt
1 tsp paprika
¼ tsp curry powder
1 Tbsp oil
1 Tbsp butter

Heat the empty browning dish on High for 6 minutes. You must have the butter and potatoes ready to go in as soon as the dish has heated. If you are a fast worker and you have your ingredients on hand you can do this while the dish heats.

Scrub or peel the potatoes, cut into 1cm cubes, then pat dry on a paper towel. Measure the flour and seasonings into a dry plastic bag, shake to mix, then add the potato cubes and shake well to coat thoroughly.

As soon as the preheating time is up pour the oil into the dish without taking it from the oven. Add the butter in several pieces, then quickly add the coated cubed potatoes.

Microwave, uncovered on High for 3 minutes. Without taking out the dish, turn the potato cubes then cook 2–3 minutes longer, until a potato cube is tender when tested.

❦ Serve hot with suitable meat or serve with pancooked bacon, tomato or mushrooms for breakfast or brunch.

Microwaved Potatoes in Coconut Cream

I have made this recipe many times in supermarkets, and am always surprised by the number of people who enjoy it so much that they rush off to buy the ingredients so they can make it themselves, straight away.

For 1–2 servings:

1 onion, chopped
4 small (new) potatoes (200g)
½–¾ cup canned coconut cream
1 tsp curry powder
¼ –½ tsp salt
½ tsp sugar
1 cup frozen peas
about 100g cauliflorets (optional)
1 cup chopped cabbage (optional)

Put the chopped onion and the unpeeled, quartered potatoes in a small microwave dish with the coconut cream, curry powder, the smaller amount of salt and the sugar. (Use the smaller amount of coconut cream if you are adding only peas.)

Cover, and microwave on High for 5 minutes, or until potatoes are barely tender, then shake to mix.

Add the frozen peas and microwave for about 3 minutes, or add a smaller amount of peas, the cauliflower and cabbage, stir to coat vegetables, then microwave for 5 minutes, stirring at least once during the cooking time.

Check that the cauliflower and cabbage are cooked to the tender-crisp stage, then taste and adjust the seasonings.

NOTE: I use new potatoes from our garden in summer, or small, pearly white Nadine potatoes at other times.

❧ Serve immediately or leave to stand, then reheat when required. This is good alone, with a green salad, or served in smaller quantities with grilled or barbecued meat or chicken.

Scalloped Potatoes

Practise until you can make this recipe without thinking twice about it. It is remarkably good, quick and easy, it looks impressive, and will stand you in good stead on many occasions, turning an ordinary meal into something special!

For 2 servings:
2–3 medium potatoes, sliced
   (300 –450g)
1 small onion, sliced
1 clove garlic, chopped (optional)
2 tsp butter
1 Tbsp water
1 Tbsp flour
½ cup milk
flavoured (or plain) salt
½ cup grated cheese
1 Tbsp chopped parsley
¼ tsp paprika

Scrub potatoes and slice them 5mm thick into a shallow, microwave casserole dish (about 20cm across) with thinly sliced onion and finely chopped garlic between layers of potato.

Add butter and water, cover, and cook on High for 5 minutes until potatoes are barely tender, shaking dish after 2–3 minutes.

Sprinkle potatoes with flour, then add the milk, and a little celery, onion, garlic, or plain salt. Shake the dish or turn potatoes to mix ingredients. Cover and cook again until sauce thickens and potatoes are perfectly tender, about 2–3 minutes. (At this stage the potatoes taste good but look boring.)

For a colourful and tasty topping, sprinkle surface evenly with grated cheese, chopped parsley, and paprika. Microwave, uncovered, just until cheese melts, about 1 minute.

❧ Serve with grilled or other meat (such as corned beef) which does not have a sauce, and with other plainly cooked vegetables.

Microwaved Herbed Potato Cake

I haven't ever made anything like this potato cake in a conventional oven, but it is easy in a microwave oven.

For 4–5 servings:

about 25g butter
4 medium potatoes (600g)
2 small onions, very finely sliced
½ cup chopped fresh parsley or other
* herbs*
2 tsp instant green herb stock
about 50g thinly sliced or grated
* cheese (½ cup)*
paprika

Melt the butter in the 6 cup microwave ring pan in which you will cook the potatoes.

Shred the scrubbed potatoes coarsely. Put into a bowl of cold water as soon as possible to prevent browning. Drain in a sieve, squeezing to remove excess water.

Mix drained potatoes with the very finely sliced (or grated) onion, the herbs, instant stock and melted butter. Press into ring pan, cover with a lid or plastic film and microwave on High for 10 minutes, or until potato is tender. Leave 2 minutes then turn out onto a flat plate.

Place cheese slices or grated cheese around top, sprinkle with paprika and microwave for about 30 seconds, until cheese melts.

VARIATION: Replace onions with 3–4 chopped spring onions, using the leaves as well as the white part.

🍎 Serve wedges, with meat or poultry and other vegetables.

Picnic Pie (see page 31)

Filo Surprise Packages (see page 36)

Leek & Potato Soup

This is a good, filling winter soup, using vegetables which are in season. My version is not traditional, but it is quick to make and it tastes very good.

For 4 - 6 servings:

50g butter
1 clove garlic, crushed
3 medium sized leeks
2–3 medium potatoes (300–450g)
4 cups water
3 tsp instant chicken stock
1 tsp instant green herb stock
1 tsp sugar
¼ –½ cup cream
salt and pepper to taste

In a large pot, melt the butter. Gently cook the garlic and thinly sliced leeks for about 10 minutes. (I use all the white part and the light green inner leek leaves, but none of the dark green parts). Do not let the vegetables brown at all during this stage. Peel the potatoes, slice thinly and add to the leeks with the water, instant stocks and sugar, and simmer for about 10 minutes until the vegetables are just tender. (Overcooking spoils the colour of the leeks.)

Blend or process the mixture, or for a chunky soup, mash with a potato masher. Add cream, according to your taste and conscience! Taste and adjust the seasoning carefully.

🍂 Serve immediately or reheat. Add a spoonful of whipped cream to each bowl for special occasions. Sprinkle with chopped chives or paprika.

Corn & Ham Chowder

A few additions can turn a packet of soup into a substantial meal. For best flavour, make this ahead of time and leave it for the flavour to develop. This is not essential though.

For 4 servings:

3 rashers bacon, chopped
   OR 100g ham pieces, chopped
1 Tbsp butter or oil
2 cloves garlic, chopped
4–6 small new potatoes
   (200 –30(g)
1 cup hot water
440g can creamed corn
1 pkt cream of chicken soup
2 cups cold water
chopped parsley, or spring onion
   leaves

In a fairly large pot, lightly brown the bacon or ham in the butter or oil. Add the garlic and cook 1 minute longer. Scrub the new potatoes and cube or quarter them. Add, with the hot water, to the pot. Cover the saucepan and simmer for 10 minutes, or until the potatoes are just tender. Add the

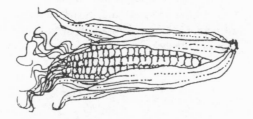

creamed corn and the packet of cream of chicken soup, mixed with the cold water. Stir over moderate heat until the mixture boils and thickens.

If serving immediately, simmer for a further 5 minutes. If you are making it ahead, turn off as soon it boils, as the mixture will cool down slowly and by the time it is reheated later it will be cooked.

Adjust seasonings, then sprinkle with chopped parsley or spring onions.

❦ Serve in large bowls with toast or bread rolls, as the main part of a meal.

Chunky Shrimp Chowder

This delicious, chunky chowder is one of my favourite soups. If you always keep a can of shrimps in your store cupboard you can make it at short notice, as a satisfying meal for unexpected guests.

For 4–6 servings:

2 medium onions, chopped
1 cup sliced celery (optional)
25g butter
1 cup hot water
1 tsp instant green herb stock
1 tsp instant chicken stock
3 medium potatoes (450g)
about 1 cup frozen mixed vegetables
*   (optional)*
200g can shrimps
2 cups milk
about 2 Tbsp cornflour
parsley and paprika for garnish

Chop the onions and celery into 1cm chunks. Cook gently in the butter, in a large covered pot, until tender but not browned. Add the water, instant stocks, and the potatoes which have been scrubbed then cut into 1cm cubes. Cover and simmer for 15 minutes, or until potatoes are tender, adding the frozen vegetables (or mixed fresh vegetables) so they will be cooked at the same time as the potatoes.

Add shrimps, liquid from can (unless it is dark in colour and very strongly flavoured) and milk, then bring to the boil. Thicken with cornflour mixed to a paste with cold water, and adjust seasonings.

TO MICROWAVE: Heat butter, onion, and celery in covered casserole on High for 3 minutes. Add boiling water, stocks and potatoes, and cook for about 6 minutes. Add rest of ingredients, except 1 Tbsp cornflour, and heat until thick, 7–10 minutes. Add remaining cornflour (mixed with water) if necessary. Boil again.

VARIATION: Replace shrimps with canned salmon, using the liquid in your chowder.

❦ Serve in large bowls with toast or bread rolls, as the main part of a meal. Serve sprinkled with parsley and paprika, and add a spoonful of lightly whipped cream for special occasions.

Sensational Salads

Hot Potato Salad

Cook 2 – 3 rashers bacon until crisp. Remove from the pan. Cook a finely chopped onion in the bacon drippings until lightly browned. Stir in 2 teaspoons flour, 1 teaspoon sugar, 2 teaspoons mixed mustard, and ¼ cup wine vinegar and stir over low heat until the dressing boils. Adjust seasoning and thin down if necessary. Slice 4 cooked new potatoes and 2 gherkins into the dressing and heat through, stirring occasionally. Sprinkle with chopped parsley, paprika and chopped cooked bacon before serving with frankfurters, sausages or cold meat.

Peanutty Potato Salad

This dressing turns potato salad into a meal. Cook a finely chopped onion and garlic clove in a frypan in 2 teaspoons oil until tender. Add 2 teaspoons brown sugar, 2 teaspoons soya sauce, 1 tablespoon lemon juice and about ¼ cup crunchy or smooth peanut butter. Stir over low heat, then add enough water and/or coconut cream to thin the sauce to pouring consistency. Add hot pepper sauce to taste.

Arrange on a bed of lettuce: sliced cooked new potatoes, 2 cm lengths of cooked chopped beans, slices of cucumber, chopped spring onions, and quartered hard boiled eggs. Pour dressing on individual servings.

American Potato Salad

A wonderful salad if made with good mayonnaise! For best flavour, moisten cooked waxy or new potatoes with equal amounts of wine vinegar and olive or other oil before they cool. Slice or cube the cooked potatoes into a bowl. For each 2 cups of potato add a chopped spring onion, 2 tablespoons chopped parsley, ¼ cup Traditional Mayonnaise, 1 teaspoon wine vinegar and ½ of a chopped hardboiled egg. Mix gently, without breaking up the potato too much. Thin if necessary with a little water, lemon juice or milk. Serve at room temperature with remaining egg, more parsley and chives.

Sensational Salads

Traditional Mayonnaise

A food processor makes wonderfully smooth mayonnaise very quickly and easily. Put in the bowl of a food processor with the metal chopping blade attached, 2 eggs, ½ cup wine vinegar, 1 teaspoon salt, 1 teaspoon sugar, 1 chopped garlic clove and 1–2 teaspoons mixed mustard. (Add fresh or dried herbs if you like.) Process to mix. With machine on, add 1½ – 2 cups of olive, canola or other oil (or a mixture) in a thin stream. Mixture will thicken as more oil is added, so stop at thickness you like. Leave to stand for added flavours to blend in. Cover and refrigerate up to 3 weeks.

In blender make only half this recipe.

Spicy Yoghurt Potato Salad

Stir this low calorie dressing through cold, cubed, cooked potatoes, for a strongly flavoured salad which is marvellous to serve with curries.

Finely chop together in a food processor, 1 large clove garlic, ½–1 small green chili, ¼ cup fresh coriander leaves, 2 spring onions, 1 teaspoon ground cumin, ½ teaspoon sugar, and ½ teaspoon salt. When finely chopped stir in 1 cup plain unsweetened yoghurt. Serve at room temperature.

Cumin Potato Salad

For an interesting dressing which adds zest to a potato salad, shake together in a screw-topped jar ½ cup olive or other oil, ¼ cup wine vinegar, 2 teaspoons ground cumin, 1 tablespoon of pulp scraped from the surface of a cut onion with a teaspoon, ¾ teaspoon salt, 2 teaspoons crumbled oreganum leaves, a very finely chopped garlic clove, black pepper and hot pepper sauce to taste.

Pour as much as you like over warm chopped or cubed potato slices and cooked peas or chopped green beans. Sprinkle with finely chopped parsley, coriander leaf, spring onions or chives.

Minted Holiday Pie

Feeding a houseful of hollow-legged children? Carry this pie to the nearest park, beach or playground or, if the weather does not co-operate, into your TV room!

For 8 –12 servings:

400g flaky pastry
6 frankfurters
5 medium potatoes, cooked
*   (about 750g)*
2 cups cooked peas, beans or leeks
1 Tbsp chopped mint
6 eggs
½ tsp salt
4–6 tomatoes (fresh or canned)

Roll out a little over half of the pastry very thinly, and line a large roasting pan with it, allowing an overhang. Roll remaining pastry very thinly to fit over the filling. Put aside.

Cut the frankfurters into small chunky pieces. Slice the potatoes over the pastry. Spread half the vegetables, and all the frankfurters around them.

Break the eggs onto a saucer. Using a fork, beat each one enough to break the yolk, and pour around the frankfurters. Save about a tablespoon of beaten egg to glaze the pastry top later. Drop the remaining vegetables evenly over the egg, then sprinkle with salt.

Slice the tomatoes and arrange evenly over the pie filling.

Spread the rolled pastry top over the filling. Dampen the overhanging bottom crust of pastry with water and gently press it down over the top crust. Brush reserved egg over surface and pierce about 12 holes in the top crust. Bake at 220°C for 15 minutes or until golden brown, then at 150°C for about 15 minutes longer.

❦ Serve the pie warm, reheated or cold, cut in squares, with carrot and celery sticks and bread rolls to fill gaps!

Picnic Pie

With a pie like this, you need only fruit and a drink to complete a picnic. For a more elaborate meal, add a cold chicken, bread rolls and a couple of salads as well.

For 6–8 servings:

about 400g flaky pastry
3 eggs
3 Tbsp milk
2 ham steaks, cubed
*   OR 4 slices cooked bacon,*
*   chopped*
2 sprigs mint
4 spring onions
4 medium new potatoes, cooked
*   (300g)*
1 cup cold cooked peas

Roll pastry thinly into two rounds. Use one to line a 23cm pie plate. Trim edges level with the edge of plate.

In a large bowl mix the eggs with the milk to combine whites and yolks. Put aside a tablespoonful for a glaze.

Add cubed ham steaks or bacon, chopped mint and spring onions, the cubed cold potatoes and peas.

Tip filling into uncooked pastry. Dampen edge of second piece of pastry and use to cover filling, folding edges under. Press edge with a fork. Decorate top with pastry scraps and glaze with reserved egg. Cut steam vents in centre.

Bake at 200°C for 30 minutes, lowering heat if pastry browns too quickly. Cool on a rack and wrap in a teatowel, rather than in plastic or foil, to keep pastry crisp.

❦ Serve as suggested above.

Neptune's Pie

The filling in this pie combines inexpensive canned smoked fish fillets and potatoes.

For about 6 servings:

1 pkt flaky pastry (400g)
2 large potatoes, cooked (500g)
300–425g can smoked fish fillets
3 eggs
½ cup chopped spring onions
1 cup grated tasty cheese

Roll out pastry into two circles, to fit a 23cm pie plate. Line it with one piece of pastry.

Cut potatoes into 1cm thick slices. Add drained, flaked fillets, the unbeaten eggs, the onions and cheese. Mix carefully, stirring eggs through the mixture without breaking up potatoes too much.

Tip into uncooked crust. Dampen surface of remaining pastry with cold water. Place damp side down over pie filling. Press outer layers together, then trim 2cm beyond pie plate edge. Fold overhang under the edge of the lower crust. Crimp edge if you like. Cut a vent in middle.

Bake at 200°C for 30–40 minutes, or until pastry is evenly browned and centre of pie has set.

🍂 Serve cold or warm as the main part of a summer meal, with one or more salads.

Jane's Potato Flan

This pie makes a good lunch dish, with a salad, or it makes a great addition to a buffet meal.

For 3 – 4 servings:

400g flaky pastry
1 cup cottage cheese
1 egg, beaten
¼ cup sour cream
1 tsp salt
2 tsp spring onions, finely chopped
1 cup mashed potato
about 2 Tbsp grated Parmesan
cheese

Line a 20cm flan tin or pie plate with flaky pastry, rolled thin.

Combine the cottage cheese, egg and sour cream in a food processor or blender, or press them through a sieve, to make a smooth mixture.

Add the salt, spring onions and mashed potato and mix again until combined. Turn potato mixture into the unbaked crust and sprinkle liberally with Parmesan cheese and bake at 220°C for 30–40 minutes, until the pastry and the top are lightly browned.

❦ Serve warm with one or more salads such as cubed tomatoes and marinated beans.

Self-Crusting Vegetable Quiche

If not over-beaten, this mixture separates during cooking, forming its own crust below a well flavoured filling.

For 4 - 6 servings:

1 large onion, chopped
2 garlic cloves, chopped
1 Tbsp butter
3 medium potatoes,
*   cooked (300–450g)*
3 eggs
¾ tsp salt
1 cup milk
½ cup self-raising flour
1 cup drained cooked asparagus,
*   spinach, mushrooms or broccoli*
1 cup grated tasty cheese

Cook the chopped onion and garlic in the butter until tender. Add the potatoes cut in 1cm cubes and cook a minute longer. Cool, then stir in the eggs, salt and milk, which have been beaten with a fork until mixed. Pour into a large bowl containing the flour, and stir with a fork until just combined. Add the chopped, well drained vegetables and cheese.

Pour into a lightly sprayed or buttered 20–23cm non-stick metal pan with a solid (not push-out) base. Garnish with sliced tomato, or thinly sliced red and green peppers if desired.

Bake at 220°C for 20–30 minutes, until lightly browned and set in the centre. Leave to stand for 5 minutes after removing from the oven.

❦ Serve hot or warm, in wedges, with a tomato or green salad, or cut in small pieces and serve as finger food.

Cheesy Onion Flan

This tasty flan makes a popular and economical family meal. Leftovers go well in school lunches too.

For 4–6 servings:

50g very cold butter
¾ cup flour
¼ cup grated cheese
2–3 Tbsp cold water
1 Tbsp oil
1 large onion, chopped
1 large clove garlic, chopped
1 tsp cumin
½ tsp oreganum
3 large new potatoes, cooked
　　(about 300g)
3 large eggs
¼ cup milk
½ tsp salt
¾ cup grated cheese
paprika

In a food processor, chop the butter into the flour. Add cheese, then the cold water drop by drop while the motor is running, until a ball has formed. Roll the pastry thinly to line a 23cm pie plate or flan tin. Chill until filling is ready.

Heat the oil in a frypan, and add the chopped onion and garlic. Cook over moderate heat until onion is transparent and lightly browned. Stir in the seasonings then the cubed potatoes. Mix well and cook until potatoes start to sizzle. Remove from heat.

Break the eggs into a bowl, add the milk and salt. Mix with a fork to blend whites and yolks then add potato mixture from pan. Stir to mix, then tip filling into the chilled pie crust.

Sprinkle surface with grated cheese and paprika, and bake at 220°C for 20 minutes or until pastry is golden brown and the filling has set.

❦ Serve warm, cold or reheated, alone or with one or more salads.

Filo Surprise Packages

The potatoes on your plate gain new importance when they are enclosed in filo pastry!

For 2 servings:

2 medium potatoes, cooked (300g)
2 Tbsp sour cream
1–2 tsp fresh herbs
¼ tsp salt
4 sheets filo pastry
edible or other ties*

*Use long chive leaves or bacon or ham rinds for edible ties, or string for ties which are removed before the packages are brought to the table.

Slice the potatoes and mix with the sour cream, herbs and salt, varying the proportions to suit yourself.

Cut the filo pastry sheets in two, so you have 4 almost square sheets for each parcel. Brush two sheets lightly with olive oil or melted butter (the entire surface need not be covered) and place unbuttered sheets on top. Place the "sandwiched" sheets for one parcel on top of each other, turning each so the corners do not sit on top of the corners of the sheet below. Pile the potato mixture in the middle. Now gather up all the corners so you have enclosed the potato in a pouch or "money bag". Tie your chosen fastening around the mouth of the package, knotting it. Gently fan out the corners attractively. Place packages on a buttered sponge roll tin, leave to stand until needed, then bake at 180°–190°C for 20–30 minutes, until evenly browned.

If preferred, wrap filling in whole "sandwiched" sheets of filo, as you would wrap up a parcel.

VARIATION: For Salmon Surprise Packages, cut into small pieces 4 slices of smoked salmon, and 2 slices of brie or camembert. Add to the above filling, with 2 teaspoons horseradish sauce. Use fresh dill or spring onions as the herbs.

❦ Serve as a luncheon dish on its own, or as a main for dinner, with fresh asparagus.

Filo Samosas

Everyone seems to enjoy the contrast of a light flaky crust with the dense, well seasoned potato filling of these little pastries. This is a simple version of a traditional Indian vegetarian snack.

For 8 small samosas (4 servings):

2 medium potatoes (300g)
1 Tbsp oil
1 medium onion, finely chopped
1½ tsp curry powder
1 tsp cumin
½ tsp garam marsala
½ tsp ground coriander
¾ cup frozen peas
1 tsp salt
½ tsp sugar
juice of ½ lemon
2 Tbsp chopped mint
   OR fresh coriander (if available)
6 sheets filo pastry
25g butter, melted

Scrub potatoes, cut into 1 cm cubes, then cook in a microwave container or pot (in a little water) until tender.

Heat the oil in a large frypan. Gently cook the onion and seasonings until onion is tender. Add the peas and 2 tablespoons of water, cover and cook for 2 minutes. Add the drained, cooked, potatoes, about ½ of the salt, sugar and lemon juice, and mix thoroughly, without breaking up the potato too much. Taste and add more salt and lemon juice if the mixture is bland. Stir in the chopped herbs.

Make a stack of three lightly buttered sheets of filo. Cut crosswise into four even strips. Put a good tablespoon of filling on the end of one strip and (see diagram) fold into a triangular parcel.

Repeat with remaining strips, filo sheets and filling mixture.

Brush lightly with melted butter. Place, on a shallow baking tray. Bake at 200°C for 10 minutes then for a further 15–20 minutes at 180°C until golden brown.

❧ Serve warm, as a snack or a light meal, at any time of day.

Pea Flour Patties

Pea flour is made from finely ground high protein, dried peas. In this eggless recipe, the raw vegetables are surrounded by batter which is flavoured with Indian spices. These patties are very popular with some but are not everybody's cup of tea!

For 4 servings:

1 cup pea flour
about ½ cup water
1 tsp turmeric
2 tsp cumin
2 tsp coriander
2 tsp garam masala
2 medium potatoes (300g)
1 onion
*1 cup frozen peas, or cauliflower
    florets etc*
oil for frying

Mix the pea flour with water and the flavourings to make a fairly stiff paste. Leave to stand for 5 minutes or longer, while you prepare the vegetables.

Scrub the potatoes, and cut them and all the other vegetables into pea-sized cubes.

Mix all the vegetables into the batter just before you intend to start cooking. They will thin down the mixture. Add extra pea flour or water to make a batter thick enough to keep the vegetables together.

Heat oil 2cm deep in a frypan and drop teaspoonfuls of mixture carefully into it. Adjust heat so patties brown nicely in about 4 minutes, then turn and cook the other side for the same time. Faster cooking will leave vegetables raw.

❧ Serve straight after cooking as finger food with a dip made from combining plain, unsweetened yoghurt, lemon juice, chopped mint, salt and a little sugar to suit your taste.

Potato Puffs

These tasty savouries are always popular, and are excellent "fillers" for teenagers. Beware, however! Straight from the oven, these are superheated. Watch that you do not burn your mouth!

For 12 savouries:

3 slices sandwich bread
1 cup mashed potato
1 cup grated tasty cheese
1 egg
1–2 Tbsp onion pulp *
1–2 rashers bacon, chopped
salt or seasoned salt
paprika

* Cut an unpeeled onion through its equator, then scrape the surface with the edge of an upside-down teaspoon.

Butter the bread lightly but evenly, cut off the crusts, then cut each slice into four small squares. Press the squares into patty pans, butter side down.

Mix mashed potatoes with cheese, egg, onion pulp and bacon. If you use a small amount of bacon, add a little salt or seasoned salt.

Put the potato mixture into the twelve uncooked bread cases and sprinkle with paprika.

Bake at 190°C for 20–30 minutes, until bread cases are light brown.

Eat when hot, or cool on a rack, then freeze for reheating later.

VARIATION: Make "giant" savouries, using a whole slice of bread in a round pie plate as the base for each.

❦ Serve with tea or coffee, mid morning or at supper time. Great with a mug of soup for a "buffet" lunch.

Bacon & Potato Savoury

This simple, but delicious summer dinner dish is quickly prepared. If I am cooking for two people and move fast, I can dig the potatoes while the bacon browns, then pick the beans while the potatoes start to cook!

For 1 serving:
2–3 rashers bacon
1 small onion
1–2 tsp butter
2–3 medium potatoes (300–450g)
about 2 Tbsp water
½ tsp instant chicken or green herb
*   stock*
*   OR ¼ tsp salt*
oreganum or cumin to taste
100–150g green beans
about 1 tsp cornflour

Chop the bacon, removing the rind, and cook in a pan until crisp, then remove most of the bacon for garnishing. Add to the remaining bacon, and drippings the chopped onion and butter, and cook until onion is transparent, and lightly browned.

Add the scrubbed, whole, halved or quartered potatoes, the water and flavourings, cover and simmer until the potatoes are tender, about 20 minutes. Add the beans, cut into 5cm lengths after 10 minutes and add a little extra water during cooking time, if necessary.

Aim to finish up with about 2 tablespoons of liquid. Thicken juices with just enough cornflour paste to coat and glaze the vegetables. Adjust seasonings.

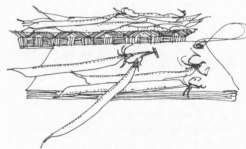

❦ Serve in large shallow bowls, sprinkled with the reserved cooked bacon, as a complete main course, with a tomato salad alongside if you choose.

Bacon and Potato Savoury

Twice Baked Stuffed Potato

Twice-Baked Stuffed Potatoes

Baked potatoes make a substantial meal when you stuff them with the contents of a can from your store cupboard.

For 4 servings:
4 large potatoes (800g)
about ¼ cup milk
½ –1 cup grated cheese
salt and pepper to taste
440g can spaghetti, baked beans,
 chili beans or chili con carne
relish or sour cream (optional)

Bake or microwave potatoes until tender (see page 8). Cut the upper third off each potato, lengthwise, and scoop the flesh carefully from all parts. Keep half of this for other use and mash the rest with milk, grated cheese, salt and pepper.

Pile into potato shells and top each one with a generous spoonful of canned spaghetti, baked beans, chili beans, or chili con carne. Reheat in oven or microwave, until potatoes and topping are hot. Depending on your filling, top potatoes with a spoonful of your favourite relish or with a teaspoon of sour cream.

❦ Serve for lunch, or with a salad or cooked vegetables for the main meal of the day.

Pizza Potatoes

Most children love the flavour of pizza. You can use the same combination of flavours in a baked potato, producing a stuffed potato which can be served as the main part of a meal.

For 1–2 servings:

1 large potato (about 200g)
1 cup grated cheese
2 spring onions, chopped
1 rasher of bacon, chopped
¼ cup chopped mushrooms
    OR red or green peppers
¼ tsp oreganum or marjoram
1 Tbsp tomato paste
liquid to thin

Choose the biggest potato in the bag! Scrub and bake in the microwave oven on High for 5–6 minutes, turning over once, or at 200°C for 1–1½ hours. (Allow 3–4 minutes standing time when microwaving.) When cooked, potato should "give" when pressed.

While potato cooks mix together in a bowl the grated cheese, chopped spring onion, bacon, mushroom or peppers, and oreganum or marjoram. Add tomato paste.

When potato is cooked, cut in half and scoop out flesh with a spoon. Mash this with the other ingredients. Add yoghurt, milk, or sour cream if mixture is dry.

Pile filling into potato halves. Garnish with a little extra bacon, pepper, olives or anchovies, if desired.

Reheat in microwave for 3–4 minutes, or in oven for 15–20 minutes.

🍎 Serve alone or with a salad.

Potato Pancakes

Potato pancakes seem especially popular with children - they enjoy their crisp texture and mild flavour.
The bacon adds interest, but can be omitted for a vegetarian dish.

For 6 servings:

2 eggs, unbeaten
2 Tbsp milk
2 rashers lean bacon, very finely
   chopped
1 onion, very finely chopped
1 tsp curry powder
1 tsp celery salt
3–4 medium potatoes (500g)
¼ cup flour

In a bowl, mix the eggs, milk, very finely chopped bacon (or ham), onion and seasonings. Stir with a fork until mixed.

Just before cooking grate the scrubbed (or thinly peeled) potatoes into the mixture, then add the flour. Heat 5mm of canola, corn or soya oil in a frypan. Cook spoonfuls of the mixture, for 3–4 minutes per side, until golden brown and cooked through.

❧ Serve alone, or with tomatoes or mushrooms for a light meal. Leave out the bacon or ham and serve with chops, steak, sausages, and vegetables for dinner.

Spanish Omelets

Although you can make lots of additions to this omelet, it tastes so good when plain that you should try it this way before you make the more elaborate versions!

For 2 servings:

3 large potatoes (600g)
3 Tbsp oil
2 eggs
½ tsp salt

Scrub and cube the potatoes. Heat the oil in a non-stick pan, then tip in the potatoes and cook until tender, about 5–10 minutes. (Potatoes need not brown).

Beat the eggs and salt with a fork. Tip the cooked potatoes into the beaten egg, then tip the mixture back into the pan, containing a little extra oil.

Cook uncovered, tilting pan occasionally, until omelet is nearly set. Slide from the pan onto a plate, then flip back into the pan to brown the second side.

VARIATIONS: Add a chopped onion to the pan with the potatoes. Mix a chopped red and or/green pepper (or chopped cooked vegetables) into the potato and uncooked egg mixture.

Slide from pan onto a plate and serve flat, not folded, cut in wedges. Add leftovers to packed lunches.

❦ Serve alone, or with salad vegetables.

Curried New Potatoes

Basic curried potatoes make an interesting change from plain new potatoes, especially when served with foods without sauce or gravy. This recipe offers you the chance to make variations on the "curried potato" theme, some of which make a complete meal.

For 4 servings:

2 Tbsp butter
1 tsp curry powder
1 onion, chopped
6 medium new potatoes (600g)
1 tsp instant chicken stock
1 tsp sugar
½ cup hot water
½ cup coconut cream or extra water

½ cup peas (optional)
¼ cup sour cream (optional)
4–6 hardboiled eggs (optional)

In a medium sized frypan, melt the butter, add curry powder and chopped onion and cook gently while you scrape the new potatoes. Cut the potatoes into halves or quarters for quicker cooking. Add to the curry mixture with the instant stock and sugar dissolved in the hot water and coconut cream if used. Cover pan and simmer gently for 15 minutes or until potatoes are tender and liquid is thick. (Watch liquid and add extra or raise heat, so you finish up with the correct consistency.) Serve or proceed as below.

Add peas and cook until peas are tender. Serve like this or add sour cream. Mixture will thin when it is added.

Cook uncovered until sauce thickens again. Serve like this or add 4–6 hardboiled eggs, sliced lengthwise. Arrange eggs cut side up and heat very gently until warm. Sprinkle with paprika if desired.

NOTE: Do not add sour cream if you have already added coconut cream to the potatoes.

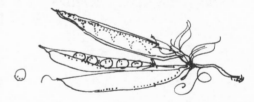

❦ Serve potatoes and peas as a vegetable, along side other foods. Serve potato and egg mixture on rice as the main part of the meal.

"Potata" Frittata

A frittata is a cross between an omelet and a crustless quiche. Make this when you want something quick and easy, or you haven't bought any special ingredients, and want to use up the small amounts of vegetables from your fridge or garden.

For 4–6 servings:

50g butter
3 onions, sliced
3–4 medium potatoes (450–600g)
2–3 zucchini, sliced (or other vegetables)
4 eggs
2 Tbsp water
½ cup grated Parmesan cheese

Melt the butter in a large non-stick pan. Cook the sliced onions in the butter, over moderate heat, until they are evenly browned. Add the sliced, unpeeled potatoes, stir well, cover the pan and cook for 15–20 minutes, stirring occasionally. After 10–15 minutes add the zucchini or other vegetables, so they will be cooked when the potatoes are.

Beat the eggs with the water and half the cheese. Pour over the pressed-down vegetable mixture, and cook over gentle heat for 10 minutes or until the sides and bottom are cooked. Sprinkle remaining Parmesan cheese over the top, then brown under a grill, until the top is set, nicely puffed and lightly browned.

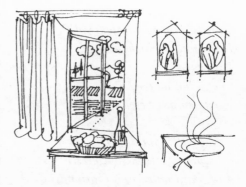

❦ Serve hot, warm or at room temperature, with crusty bread and salad. Pack leftovers for picnics or in school lunches.

Swiss Potato Cake

*I love Swiss Potato Cakes! I am sure that my untraditional version would horrify a dedicated Swiss cook,
but it works, is easy, and tastes very good.*

For 1 serving:

*2 medium potatoes, grated
(about 300g)
about 25g butter, melted
2 tsp oil
about ½ cup grated cheese
2 tsp finely chopped herbs
½ cup sautéed mushrooms*

Shred the scrubbed potatoes quite coarsely with a sharp cutter e.g. the blade of a food processor which makes long shreds. Plunge them into cold water, leave to stand for at least 5 minutes, then drain in a colander and pat dry on a paper towel or teatowel. Melt the butter in a fairly large pot or bowl, then toss the potato in it, lightly coating as many pieces as possible.

Heat the oil in a small non-stick pan. Coat the whole pan, then add the potato, pressing it down quite firmly. Put the lid lightly on the pan, and cook the cake over moderate heat for about 15 minutes or until golden brown. Slide the potato cake out of the pan onto the lid or a plate, then flip it back into the pan, so the uncooked side is down.

Cook the second side for about 10 minutes, again with the lid ajar. During the last 3 minutes put the grated cheese mixed with whatever fresh, chopped herbs you have and like, over the central part, top with the sautéed mushrooms, and let the cheese melt slightly. Slide the potato cake onto a plate, with the cheese and mushroom topping uppermost.

❦ Serve as the main part of a meal straight after cooking, with a side salad and bread roll, if you like.

Curried Sausage Pie

Everyone in my house loves this recipe. The woman who sent it to me told me that she had several teenage sons.
I can just imagine them sitting round the table, happily tucking in!

For 4–6 servings:

4–6 medium potatoes (about 1kg)
2 medium onions
1kg sausagemeat
1 Tbsp curry powder
2 Tbsp brown sugar
400g can apple sauce
*   OR 2 cups cooked apple*
1 Tbsp butter
freshly ground black pepper
½ cup of milk
½–1 cup grated cheese

Thinly peel potatoes, cut in even-sized pieces, and cook in a pot of lightly salted water.

Slice the onions. Spread half of the onion pieces into a roasting pan or large shallow baking dish. Working with wet hands, form the sausagemeat into walnut sized sausage shapes or "blobs" and arrange these over the onion pieces, in one layer. Cover with the remaining onion.

Mix the curry powder and brown sugar and sprinkle evenly over the sausages, then spread with the apple sauce or the drained cooked apple.

Drain and mash the cooked potatoes with the butter, pepper and milk. Spread the mashed potato evenly over the sausages, swirl or roughen the top attractively, then sprinkle with the grated cheese.

Bake, uncovered, at 180°C for 1 hour.

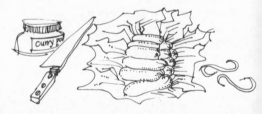

🍎 Serve with cooked vegetables or salad for the main meal of the day.

Curried Sausage Pie

Potatoes to die for

Potatoes to Die For!

*This potato dish is really delicious. I always feel a certain degree of guilt as I pour in the sour cream,
but I justify it by the fact that I cook this only as an occasional treat.*

For 4 main course servings:

10 medium potatoes (1½ kg)
3 large cloves garlic
¼ cup flour
½ tsp salt
2 cups low-fat sour cream
½ cup milk
200g gruyere cheese

to die....for... sinfully woundrous.... wow!

Scrub or peel the potatoes, cut into 5mm slices, and drop them into a large container of cold water. Check to make sure that all the slices are separated. Transfer the drained potatoes to a microwave dish or oven bag, cover bowl or tie bag loosely, and microwave until the potatoes are tender, about 15 minutes on High.

Make the sauce while the potatoes cook. Chop the garlic finely, then add to it, mixing until smooth, the flour, salt, sour cream and milk. Butter or spray an ovenproof dish, about 23 x 30cm. Overlap half the potatoes in it, drizzle half the sour cream mixture over, then grate on almost half the cheese. Repeat with the remaining ingredients, then grate the rest of the cheese evenly all over the top.

Bake uncovered at 180°C for about 30 minutes, until the mixture feels firm and the topping golden brown. Leave to stand in a warm place for 5–10 minutes before serving.

VARIATION: For an extra-special treat, top with 200–300g flaked, hot-smoked salmon, breaking it into flakes and strewing it over the browned surface of the potatoes as soon as you take them from the oven.

❦ Serve as the main part of the meal, with a mixed green salad in a tart, mustardy dressing.

Vegetarian Shepherd's Pie

This recipe is suitable for vegetarians, but meat-eaters feel happy about it, too. A shepherd's pie will "pass muster" with no meat in it, but it certainly couldn't exist without its delicious potato top.

For 4–6 main course servings:

6 medium potatoes (about 1kg)
2 Tbsp butter
1 cup grated cheese
milk
2 large onions
2 Tbsp butter
1 red or green pepper
3 Tbsp flour
1 tsp instant vegetable stock
1 tsp each dried basil, oreganum, paprika and dark soya sauce
1½ cups water, beer, wine or bean liquid
2 Tbsp tomato concentrate
440g can red kidney beans

Simmer peeled potatoes until tender. Drain, and mash with butter, half the grated cheese, and enough milk for a good consistency. After mashing, beat with a fork until light and fluffy.

In a large pot or pan, cook the chopped onions in the butter until tender and medium brown. Add the chopped pepper and flour, and stir until the flour has browned lightly. Add the remaining ingredients except the beans then bring to the boil, stirring constantly, before adding the drained beans.

Spread the mixture into a lightly sprayed pan about 20 x 25cm and cover with the mashed potato, spreading it so all the beans are covered. Sprinkle the remaining grated cheese over the surface. If not using immediately, refrigerate.

When required, cook uncovered at 180°C for 20–30 minutes, or in a microwave oven until the bottom centre feels hot to your hand. Brown the top under a grill if necessary.

VARIATION: For a traditional Shepherds Pie (for meat eaters) replace the beans with 2 cups of finely chopped cold roast lamb or hogget. (Make sure meat is chopped so it retains some texture. Chop into 2cm pieces before food processing a little bit at a time.)

❦ Serve with a green vegetable such as brussel sprouts, beans or broccoli.

Spiced Potatoes

When you cook new potatoes in a spicy, coconut cream sauce, you make an interesting meal.
The mixture will not be "hot" unless you add the chili powder.

For 4 large servings:

1 large onion, chopped

2 cloves garlic, chopped

2 Tbsp butter or oil

1/2 tsp each ground cumin, cardamom and coriander

1/4 tsp ground celery seed

1/4 tsp ground cloves

1/8 tsp chili powder (optional)

1 tsp turmeric

410g can coconut cream

4–5 new potatoes (600–700g)

3 cups frozen peas or chopped green beans

1 Tbsp sugar

1/2 tsp salt

Put the chopped onion and garlic into a large frying pan with the butter or oil. Cook gently for 4–5 minutes, until transparent and lightly browned. Add the next 7 spices and stir over low heat for 2–3 minutes longer. Add the coconut cream and bring to the boil.

Scrub or scrape the potatoes and halve or quarter them if large. Add to pan, cover and simmer, turning occasionally, until potatoes are just tender, usually 15–20 minutes. Add the peas or beans (chopped in 2cm lengths), the sugar and salt and cook a few minutes longer until peas (or beans) are tender. Adjust thickness of sauce by boiling briskly for a few minutes if too thin, or adding a little water if it too thick. Taste and adjust seasonings if necessary.

VARIATION: Add 1/2–1 cup of toasted cashew nuts just before serving.

❦ Serve alone or on rice, with your choice of curry side dishes.

Holiday Hash

I don't ever think we should feel apologetic when we cook something like this for a holiday meal. This is a good, one pan meal, but it needs a little organisation ahead. You can precook the potatoes in a microwave.

For 4 servings:

4 large potatoes, cooked (800g)
1–2 cups cubed cooked meat or
    luncheon sausage
¼ cup chopped gherkins, cucumber
    or other pickle
4 spring onions, chopped
¼ cup chopped parsley

Roughly chop, or mash with a fork, the cooked potatoes. Mix them with the finely cubed meat, chopped gherkins or pickle, white and green parts of the spring onions and parsley. If you use meat that has not been salted, you may want to add a sprinkling of celery or garlic salt.

Heat a 20–23cm non-stick frypan. Add 1–2 tablespoons of butter or oil, swirl it around the pan to coat the bottom and sides, then quickly, before it burns, add the potato mixture. Cover pan for more even heating, if possible.

Cook over a moderate heat until the hash forms a crust all round the bottom and sides. (This may take 20–30 minutes.) Carefully run a knife around it so it does not stick, then slip it out onto a plate, so the uncooked side is still up. Invert it into the pan again, with a little extra butter or oil, then cook the second side.

NOTE: If the potato and meat mixture looks dry before it is cooked, add a little milk, to dampen it so it will stay together during cooking.

❦ To serve, cut into quarters. It is nice with tomatoes and coleslaw or a lettuce salad.

Oakhill Potatoes

This popular potato dish has stolen the show at many a party over the years! It does require some time and effort but you can make it an advance, and refrigerate it until needed.

For 4 - 6 servings:

4 large cooked potatoes (800g)
2 hardboiled eggs
1–2 rashers bacon
1 onion
50g butter
¼ cup flour
1 tsp dry mustard
1 tsp salt
2 cups milk
½ cup grated cheese
1 Tbsp butter
1 cup fresh breadcrumbs

Slice the cooked potatoes into a shallow sprayed or buttered baking dish. Add chopped eggs.

Chop the bacon and onion and cook in the first measure of butter in a fairly large pot until the onion is transparent.

Stir in the flour, mustard and salt, add 1 cup of milk then bring to the boil, stirring constantly. Add remaining milk and boil again. Stir in grated cheese. If sauce seems too thick to pour easily, thin it with extra milk. Pour over potatoes, covering the entire surface.

Top with buttered crumbs made by melting the second measure of butter and stirring in the crumbs.

Bake uncovered at 180°C for 30–45 minutes, until heated through and lightly browned.

VARIATION: For a vegetarian meal, leave out the bacon and use twice as much cheese.

❦ Serve as part of a buffet dinner, or as a family meal, with a salad and bread rolls.

Murphy's Moussaka

This is my favourite Moussaka. I make it untraditionally (but more quickly) starting with sliced cooked potatoes. I use tomatoes with Italian-style herbs added, but you can use a can of whole tomatoes and add basil, thyme and oreganum if you prefer to.

For 6 servings:

500g mince
2 large onions, finely chopped
2 Tbsp oil
½ tsp salt
2 Tbsp flour
1 can Italian Seasoned Tomatoes
5 medium potatoes, cooked (750g)

Sauce:
2 Tbsp flour
2 Tbsp butter
½ tsp freshly grated nutmeg
1 cup milk
1 cup grated cheese
1 egg, beaten

In a large frypan over high heat brown the meat and onions in the oil, stirring frequently. Stir in the salt and flour, and cook briefly before adding the tomatoes. Heat until the mixture boils and thickens.

Cut the cooked potatoes lengthwise into 5mm slices.

To prepare the sauce melt the butter, add the flour and seasonings and cook briefly, stirring constantly. Add half the milk and stir continuously until the sauce thickens. Add the rest of the milk and continue to stir until sauce boils and thickens. Remove from the heat and stir

in the grated cheese, and the egg.

Spray or butter a shallow oven-proof dish of about 10–12 cup capacity and cover the base with a third of the sliced potato. Cover with half the mince, the next third of the potatoes, then the rest of the mince. Cover this with the remaining sliced potatoes. Press down fairly flat. Pour the cheese sauce over the top layer of potato and bake at 180°C for 20–30 minutes.

❦ Serve alone, or with a cooked green vegetable or a crisp salad for a main meal.

Party Potatoes

Here is a "shortcut" recipe which may help you when you are preparing a meal for a crowd.
The buttery herbed coating disguises the flavour and appearance of the canned potatoes.

For 40 servings:

*2–3 large cans cooked potatoes ***
6–8 Tbsp melted butter
about 1 cup fresh herbs, chopped
*   eg. parsley, chives, thyme and*
*   oreganum OR parsley, chives*
*   and dill*

*Ask your grocer if he will get you large cans of small potatoes in brine. Each 3kg can should contain about 45 small potatoes. Allow about 2–3 potatoes per person, depending on the age and appetites of your guests.

Put half a can of drained potatoes in a covered microwave dish (or large tough oven bag) with $\frac{1}{2}$ cup of the liquid from the can, and heat through on High for 9–10 minutes.

Drain potatoes, turn in a little melted butter, allowing 1–2 tablespoons per half can of potatoes, then sprinkle generously with about $\frac{1}{4}$ cup of very finely chopped fresh herbs. (Chop dry herbs in food processor for best results.) Mix gently to coat evenly. Repeat this process with remaining potatoes.

If you cannot microwave the potatoes just before you need them as above, then put them in "oven" or "roasting" bags, in an insulated "chilly bin" type container,

for up to an hour. Transfer to serving dishes just before the meal. (Roasting bags are light, compact, unbreakable and easily transportable. Close them loosely with rubber bands when microwaving. Use twist ties if heating bags of potatoes in a regular oven.)

NOTE: Leftover canned potatoes may be refrigerated in plastic bags for 3–4 days.

Cooked potatoes should never be left "standing around" for long without refrigeration, especially in warm weather.

❦ Serve as part of a buffet meal, as you would freshly cooked new potatoes.
Use leftovers in potato salads, in scalloped potato dishes, or as sautéed potatoes.

Potato Pizzaz

POTATO POWER

Potatoes not only taste good, but are good for you! They contain many nutrients per calorie, and are high in complex carbohydrates. Nutritionists tell us to eat more of them! Since they are so well-liked, and are usually cheaper per kilogram than other foods, we can enjoy them regularly.

A plainly cooked 100 gram potato contains almost no fat and less than 100 calories. When you cook potatoes in oil or butter, however, or add butter or

cream before serving them, remember that you are adding fat and calories!

CHOOSING POTATOES

All potatoes are not the same. Different types vary in size, shape, colour, flavour and texture.

These differences are due partly to the variety of the potatoes, but also to the place where they were grown. The type and texture of the soil, its wetness, dryness, the day and night time temperatures, and many other factors affect potatoes.

This means that although you may always buy your favourite potato variety, the potatoes you buy today are unlikely to be exactly the same as those you bought a month ago, grown in another place, under different conditions.

Don't let these minor differences worry you, however. If you find your potatoes break up a little as they boil,

enjoy them mashed. If they are waxier than usual, slice them for salads and sautées.

Look for potatoes which are named, packed and labelled so you know exactly what you are getting and where they were grown. Choose potatoes which have been carefully sized and cleaned, and are free from bruises, cuts and blemishes. These may seem to cost a little more, but you will have little wastage and will enjoy working with, and eating them. The more you buy such potatoes, the more you are encouraging high potato standards.

STORING POTATOES

If you buy a large bag of maincrop potatoes, you will probably pay much

Potato Pizzaz

less, per kilo, for them. Stored properly, they will keep for weeks. Take potatoes out of plastic bags as soon as you get them home, and store them in a cool, dry place, away from bright light. Do not refrigerate raw potatoes. New potatoes are best bought in amounts you will use in a few days.

NEW POTATOES

Freshly dug, waxy new potatoes are a seasonal treat, to be selected carefully, transported and cooked gently, and served with loving care! Look for small boxes of these in season, at good green-grocers' shops and at supermarkets — perhaps even by mail-order! Compared with other foods they are an inexpensive treat. Their skins should rub or scrape off easily if they are freshly dug.

NON-STICK PANS

If you enjoy potatoes with crisp golden crusts, invest in a non-stick frying pan. As well as making your cooking easier, a non-stick pan will let you produce golden crusty potatoes with much less added fat. Choose a pan with a lid, or find another lid which will fit it, for greatest versatility. For a large family, a large covered non-stick pan with a heavy base which spreads the heat is best.

MICROWAVING POTATOES

Many potato dishes microwave very quickly and well (see pages 18-22.) For good microwaved potatoes, plain or fancy, cook to the right stage. Undercooked microwaved potatoes are hard, and overcooked ones have a shrunken appearance. Do not blame the microwave oven for these faults!

GREEN POTATOES

Potatoes which have been exposed to sunlight while growing or during storage may have a green colour. Do not cook, and never eat potatoes with green flesh. Do not mistake the slightly yellowish flesh of some potato varieties with green potatoes.

COOKING TIMES VARY

Some potatoes take longer to cook than others. This is not a fault — just allow for it. Always test to see whether potatoes are ready, rather than using a specific time.

Index

Index

Knives by Mail Order

For the past 17 years I have imported my favourite, very sharp kitchen knives from Switzerland. These keep their edges well, are easy to sharpen, and a pleasure to use. These knives are extremely sharp. Please use them with care until you are used to this!

VEGETABLE KNIFE $8.00 Pointed, straight edged, 85mm blade, in a plastic sheath. Useful for peeling vegetables and cutting small objects.

UTILITY KNIFE $9.00 Pointed 103mm blade which slopes back, in a plastic sheath. Use for boning chicken and meat and general kitchen use.

SERRATED KNIFE $9.00 Rounded end, 110mm serrated knife in a plastic sheath. This never needs sharpening, will stay sharp for years, and is unbelievably useful for slicing steak, bread and fresh baking, tomatoes and fruit, etc.

THREE PIECE SET $17.00 Serrated knife (as above), 85mm blade vegetable knife with pointed tip, and (right-handed) potato peeler, all with black dishwasher-proof handles, together in a white plastic pack.

GIFT BOX KNIFE SETS $38.00 Five knives and a (right-handed) potato peeler. Contains straight bladed vegetable knife, blade 85mm; serrated edged vegetable knife, blade 85mm; small utility knife with a pointed tip blade 85mm; small serrated utility 85mm; larger rounded end serrated knife 110mm (same as above) ("Straight edge" means that blade is in line with handle.) Attractive pack.

SERRATED CARVING KNIFE $25.00 Cutting edge 21 cm, overall length 33 cm. Black, moulded dishwasher-proof handle. Cuts beautifully, and does not require sharpening. (Sharpening wears down the serrations.) In sheath.

STEEL $20.00 20 cm blade, 34 cm total length, black dishwasher-proof handle. Produces excellent results.

KNIFE SHARPENER $30.00 This sits on a bench, and is held safely, without slipping, with one hand while you draw a CLEAN knife (of any length) through it with your other hand. Easy to use, with two rotating sharpening disks of synthetic ruby. When knife is held vertically, discs are at ideal angle to sharpen it to a fine point. Dishwasher-proof. Do not use with serrated knives. This is excellent if you have trouble using a steel efficiently.

For each order (any number of knives) please add $3.00 for packing and postage. All prices include GST. These prices apply until the end of 1995.

Please send cheque with your order to:

Alison Holst Mail Orders
PO Box 17016
Wellington